MRJC
4/14

Words I Know

A Pocket Full of Nouns

by Bette Blaisdell

Content Consultant:
Terry Flaherty, PhD
Professor of English
Minnesota State University, Mankato

CAPSTONE PRESS
a capstone imprint

A+ Books are published by Capstone Press,
1710 Roe Crest Drive, North Mankato, Minnesota 56003
www.capstonepub.com

Library of Congress Cataloging-in-Publication Data
Blaisdell, Bette.
A pocket full of nouns / by Bette Blaisdell.
       pages cm.—(A+ books. Words I know.)
Summary: "Full-color photographs and rhyming text introduce and define a variety of nouns"—Provided by publisher.
ISBN 978-1-4765-3938-6 (library binding)
ISBN 978-1-4765-5098-5 (paperback)
ISBN 978-1-4765-5943-8 (ebook PDF)
1. English language—Nouns—Juvenile literature. I. Title.
PE1201.B55 2014
428.2—dc23   2013035672

Editorial Credits
Jill Kalz, editor; Juliette Peters, designer; Svetlana Zhurkin, media researcher; Kathy McColley, production specialist

Photo Credits
Alamy: Idamini, cover; Juliette Peters, 15 (top); Shutterstock: a. v. ley, 12 (top), AKaiser (swirls), 2–3, 4–5, 32, Alan Bailey, 24 (left), Aletia, 30–31, Alexander Ozerov, 18 (top), Alfio Scisetti, 1, 4 (top), 5 (top), alslutsky, 26 (top), Andresr, 25 (bottom), Andrew Burgess, 7 (top), Anna Sedneva, 23 (top), auremar, 8 (left), Camilo Torres, 6, Charles Brutlag, 28 (bottom), Charles L. Bolin, 12 (bottom), Daniel Prudek, 27 (top), David Lee, 24 (right), Dmitrydesign, 21 (bottom), Dustin Dennis, 29 (bottom), effe45, 11 (top), esfera, 8–9, Fer Gregory, 30 (bottom), Gunnar Rathbun, 17 (bottom), holbox, 9, Hurst Photo, 29 (top), Ilike, 5 (bottom), Jeff McGraw, 17 (top), Jennifer Stone, 13 (top), Jo Crebbin, 16 (top), joyfull, 19, kamnuan, 27 (bottom), Maksym Bondarchuk, 4 (bottom front), Mikhail Melnikov, 26 (bottom), MO_SES, 21 (top), Mr. Suttipon Yakham, 7 (bottom), Pagina, 16 (bottom), Peter Kunasz, 13 (bottom), Phil McDonald, 28 (top), Piti Tan, 10 (bottom), Robyn Mackenzie, 23 (bottom), Rocky33, 25 (top), Rudolf Tepfenhart, 4 (bottom back), Sea Wave, 22 (right), sippakorn, 11 (bottom), Sofiaworld, 14, STILLFX, 12–13 (back), Svetlana Foote, 22 (left), Thomas M. Perkins, 20 (bottom), Todd Shoemake, 18 (bottom), udeyismail, 20 (top), Vladislav Lebedinski, 10 (top), Wiktory, 15 (bottom)

Note to Parents, Teachers, and Librarians
This Words I Know book uses full-color photographs and a nonfiction format to introduce the concept of language and parts of speech. A Pocket Full of Nouns is designed to be read aloud to a pre-reader or to be read independently by an early reader. Photographs help listeners and early readers understand the text and concepts discussed. The book encourages further learning by including the following sections: Table of Contents, Read More, and Internet Sites. Early readers may need assistance using these features.

Printed in the United States of America in Stevens Point, Wisconsin.
092013   007773WZS14

Table of Contents

What's a Noun?

Is it a **dentist**?
Or a **desert**?
How about a **dandelion**?

Yes! It's all of these!

A **noun** is a part of speech that names a person, place, or thing.

There are two kinds of nouns: common and proper. Common nouns name a general person, place, or thing. They begin with a lowercase letter. Examples of common nouns include *brother, park,* and *holiday.*

Proper nouns name a specific person, place, or thing. They begin with a capital letter. *Carson, Central Park,* and *Valentine's Day* are proper nouns.

What nouns do you keep in *your* pocket?

More Than Cats and Dogs

Some pets are big, and some are small.
It doesn't matter. We love them all!

goldfish
crab
rabbit
gerbil

spider
iguana
ferret
turtle

hamster

snail

chinchilla

frog

python

parakeet

finch

hedgehog

On the Job

When I grow up, what will I be?
What do you think of President ME?

dancer

artist

sheriff

physician

farmer

dentist

athlete

magician

astronaut
actor teacher
electrician

firefighter clown soldier
musician

Sweet Sounds

Drums, rattles, and whistles made of clay.
Which of these instruments can you play?

recorder
flute
harmonica
banjo

clarinet
guitar
oboe
piano

trombone
trumpet
tuba
saxophone

cello
ukelele
violin

xylophone

America, the Beautiful

Not all 50 states are listed here,
but each deserves a patriotic cheer!

Minnesota
California
Georgia

New Mexico

Kentucky
New Hampshire
Oklahoma
Idaho

Maryland
Washington
Wisconsin
Ohio

Mississippi
Illinois
Texas

Colorado

How Does Your Garden Grow?

When a gardener has the tools she needs,
she can grow big veggies from little seeds.

gloves

shears

tillers

stakes

hoes

shovels

trowels

rakes

carrots
lettuce
broccoli
tomatoes

spinach
onions
peapods
potatoes

Whoohoo for the Zoo!

A day at the zoo is a day of fun.
Let's name the animals, one by one.

lemur
cheetah
penguin
rhino

tortoise
gorilla
tiger
flamingo

16

wallaby
giraffe
macaw
caribou

dolphin
sloth
otter
emu

Weather Wise

Take a peek outside. Is the sky blue or gray?
What will the weather bring today?

sunshine
storm
shower
rainbow

lightning
drought
hail
tornado

mist

drizzle

sleet

rain

cloud

flood

fog

hurricane

19

Catch a Cab

How can you get from here to there?
Stay on the ground, or take to the air!

tractor
balloon
sleigh

motorbike

scooter
wagon
taxi

trike

20

canoe
sailboat
helicopter

airplane

kayak
skateboard
snowmobile
train

21

Happy and Healthy

Pack a lunch with foods that are yummy,
and soon you'll have a party in your tummy!

cucumbers
peppers
bananas

cheese

strawberries
celery
grapes
peas

apples
yogurt
blueberries
beans

oranges
crackers
cherries

greens

Go, Team!

Show your teammates what you've got.
Over here! I'm open! I'll take a shot!

skates
mitt
puck
basketball

cleats   **bat**   **tee**
baseball

jersey
helmet
hoop
football

goal
racquet
rink
volleyball

An Insect's World

They creep. They fly. They scurry too.
Which of these insects are new to you?

ladybug
mosquito
moth

dragonfly

ant
scorpion
beetle
horsefly

grasshopper

honeybee

cockroach

centipede

butterfly

cicada

flea

millipede

Summer Treats

Beneath the sun so high and bright,
we laugh, we play, we fly a kite!

marshmallows

fireworks
Popsicles
pie

pineapple
hot dogs

Fourth
of July

campfire
swimsuit
flip-flops
lemonade

watermelon
sprinkler
sandbox
parade

Sweet Dreams

The day is done, but no need to be blue.
Your soft, comfy bed is waiting for you.

sunset

cricket

streetlight

firefly

bathtub

toothbrush

slippers

lullaby

pajamas
nightgown
blanket
twilight

moonbeam
quilt
pillow

starlight

Read More

Doyle, Sheri. *What Is a Noun?* Parts of Speech. North Mankato, Minn.: Capstone Press, 2013.

Murray, Kara. *Nouns and Pronouns.* Core Language Skills. New York: PowerKids Press, 2014.

Riggs, Kate. *Nouns.* Grammar Basics. Mankato, Minn.: Creative Education, 2013.

Internet Sites

FactHound offers a safe, fun way to find Internet sites related to this book. All of the sites on FactHound have been researched by our staff.

Here's all you do:

Visit *www.facthound.com*

Type in this code: 9781476539386

Check out projects, games and lots more at
www.capstonekids.com